P9-CBI-456

aMAZEing

Organizational Teams

*Navigating 7 Critical Attributes for
Cohesion, Productivity and Resilience*

Ellen Burts-Cooper

authorHOUSE®

AuthorHouse™
1663 Liberty Drive
Bloomington, IN 47403
www.authorhouse.com
Phone: 1 (800) 839-8640

© 2016 Ellen Burts-Cooper. All rights reserved.

No part of this book may be reproduced, stored in a retrieval system, or
transmitted by any means without the written permission of the author.

Published by AuthorHouse 05/10/2016

ISBN: 978-1-5246-0813-2 (sc)
ISBN: 978-1-5246-0812-5 (e)

Library of Congress Control Number: 2016907637

Print information available on the last page.

Any people depicted in stock imagery provided by Thinkstock are models,
and such images are being used for illustrative purposes only.
Certain stock imagery © Thinkstock.

This book is printed on acid-free paper.

Because of the dynamic nature of the Internet, any web addresses or
links contained in this book may have changed since publication and
may no longer be valid. The views expressed in this work are solely those
of the author and do not necessarily reflect the views of the publisher,
and the publisher hereby disclaims any responsibility for them.

This book is dedicated to all of those who know
that working collaboratively can produce something
bigger than we each can individually.

Contents

Motivation for the Work

The aMAZEing team is for collaborative spirits who want to understand team dynamics in the workplace.

My team and I have written this book in large part because of the enormous enthusiasm we have received for both our training on this topic and our aMAZEing Team Building Experience. We have found that most teams are operating at about 70 percent productivity, and by and large, the go-to solution to increase productivity is to simply have people work more hours. This is not the answer! We believe that moving teams to get that additional 30 percent is done not by having them work more hours, but by tapping into their passions, encouraging them to continuously exceed expectations, and creating an environment in which they can do their best work.

I have successfully helped teams navigate the maze of complexities in a number of industries, including retail services, manufacturing, financial services, nonprofit, professional services, research and development, global sales, commercialization, project management, training and development, IT, and small business teams.

Currently I spend about 20 percent of my time in educational institutions and universities studying the latest research and theory on teams; over 80 percent of my time and my team's time is spent visiting organizations across multiple industries, assisting with issues related to the seven team attributes we'll explore in this book. The information we share with you is not just theoretical, but is truly an applied approach. From court systems, to healthcare, manufacturing, financial services, social services, and retail management, to sales, our team has been there helping hundreds of teams that have, through feedback, direct and independent evaluation, and observation, noted significant improvements. Putting the seven critical team attributes into a manuscript allows us to reach even more teams, giving them the knowledge they need to put these simple, yet effective, tools into action to deliver even more value back to their organizations.

My passion to *improve* fuels my pursuit to move teams to the next level. We work so much of our time in teams that it is critical that we get people to work together as cohesive units and collaborate in a way that allows for optimal productivity. Some teams are working more than 90 percent of their time in teams and still focus on being individual contributors. Some systems are simply not set up to encourage teamwork. Your organization has to use the attributes described in this book to be very intentional about getting people to change their mind-set to think about self *and* others as they approach their work. Oftentimes teams are accused of working in silos because they lack the cross functional communication and collaboration to really optimize results for the customer. Customers don't typically think in terms of departments, so teams have to learn to work collectively as one large unit even if the work is divided into subteams.

In turn, leaders must understand these attributes in order to encourage their teams to think about the collective good versus simply the individual contribution to work activity and projects. It's tough because we are typically measured on our individual performance but we work most of our time on teams. So there has to be a way for organizations to set up the metrics and performance evaluations such that team collaboration is a heavily weighted component. We are rarely able to deliver to a customer an independent body of work that will be more optimal than one having the additional brainpower of others as a part of the outcome.

Teams many times worry about competition. There's also a healthy level of competition that allows for subteams to have wins but not at the expense of wins for the larger collective team. In many cases this behavior of thinking about self and others in our decision-making process will require a very intentional focus.

The purpose of this body of work on teams is to encourage collaborative behavior. Most people find it fun to have the energy of others as a part of their daily work activity. As humans we thrive on interacting with others, and working on teams allows us to do so in a manner that also increases productivity for the organization.

The overall goal is really to increase *productivity* for organizations, ensure that teams are *cohesive* and genuinely enjoy engaging together, and ensure that teams are also *resilient* and able to sustain high morale for extended periods of time.

Thus, our goal is to achieve *productivity, cohesion,* and *resilience* to deliver optimal performance through superior team engagement.

Organizational Team Dynamics

Organizational teams come in a variety of types and sizes. However, several elements provide a firm foundation for a basic definition. These elements include teams (a) being comprised of two or more individuals, (b) existing to perform tasks for the benefit of the organization, (c) sharing one or more common goals, and (d) interacting in some form (face-to-face or via technology).

The use of teams has become an important factor in the success of organizations around the globe. Teams benefit organizations by combining skilled people in order to operate more efficiently and effectively than individuals working alone.

Organizations often turn to teams to make the most efficient use of their employees and other resources. While larger organizations may have multiple departments and teams, small organizations may be made up entirely of a single team, on which everyone works jointly to achieve a common goal. In the US organizations that we work with and visit, we are finding that nearly 82 percent of their employees' time is spent working on teams, regardless of industry.

Organizations, teams, and individuals are connected by a multilevel system. Individuals come together to form teams, and teams work together within the larger multilevel system. Forming an effective team is more complex than simply throwing a group of people together, assigning them a task, and hoping for the best; effective teams are generally made up of various personalities. The team-selection process needs to be structured so that it is not biased toward one personality type. An effective team needs both thoughtful, detail-oriented individuals and outgoing, insightful individuals.

The organization needs to first determine what the skills, knowledge, and attitudes of potential team members should be. Then potential team members can be interviewed and their skills and knowledge assessed. A few questions that the interview process should cover follow:

- What strengths will the individual bring to the team?
- What area of opportunity is she or he willing to work on in the new role?

- What problem-solving style and skills does the individual utilize in a given situation?
- Can he or she share information in an effective manner?
- Does the individual have good listening skills?
- Can the individual receive and provide constructive feedback?
- Does the individual fit with the organization and department that he or she applied for?

Remember: *Teams do not behave; individuals do*—but how the individuals behave affects the cohesiveness, productivity, and resiliency of the team and the organization overall. What does it mean for a team to be cohesive, productive, and resilient? A *cohesive* team can stick together to work toward and achieve a common goal. A *productive* team will generate value-added outcomes and results for the organization. Lastly, a *resilient* team is a team that is sustainable, one that can last through various phases of organizational growth and development.

Teams and Organizational Culture

For the past fourteen years, I have been collecting data and working with and studying the most effective teams in various industries. Through my research, I began to notice that seven attributes continued to surface in the most productive teams. Although my research is ongoing, it is my belief that without these attributes, it is impossible to influence a positive and collaborative culture in our organizations. Why is that? Because *our organizational culture is created by teams of individuals assembled to do the work of the organization. The environment we create through these teams really matters.* I am asked all the time how to change organizational culture. Well, that requires each individual who is a part of the culture to make a small change. The overall culture is a compilation of the behavior of all individual members. Each person has to make an effort to intentionally and consistently model the desired behavior.

The fact is that teams exist everywhere and are not going away. And if teams play such a huge role in creating our organizational culture, then I have to ask, *Why aren't we* intentionally and consistently *devoting more of our time and energy to ensure that they are effective?*

The Attributes of a Cohesive, Productive, and Resilient Team

So, what are these seven attributes that make a team cohesive, productive, and resilient? Take a look at the list below.

1. A core foundation of **trust**
2. An **appreciation** for each team member
3. Effective, efficient, and resonant **communication**
4. **Behavior management**
5. Effective and efficient **meeting management** strategy
6. Solid **problem solving and decision making**
7. A focus on **creativity and ideation**

~

Teamwork drives culture.
Culture drives productivity.

*For optimal productivity, the
people must be effective, the
processes must be efficient, and
the teams must be **cohesive**
and **engaged**.*

Dreaming: The Birth of the aMAZEing Team-Building Experience

In the fall of 2012, I had an interesting day that sparked my intentional focus into team dynamics in the workplace.

My morning started out like any other day, checking my calendar to confirm my client visits (I had a hospital, a school, a small retail outlet, and a manufacturing plant) and then reciting my daily mantra, "Make today better than yesterday." Little did I know that this day would actually change the focus of my work. Despite the different challenges each client faced, as I went on my visits, I began to notice a common thread woven throughout: their teams were in trouble.

At the hospital, I noticed a physician talking to a nurse in such a way that I was embarrassed for both of them. They were on the same team; how could this be the case? Given what was at stake, I was fearful of *what could happen if they were not working as a unit.*

At the school, two teachers were going back and forth and using inappropriate language in front of a fifth-grade student. The student was laughing, and the teachers never noticed. I asked the student to go back into the classroom and asked the teachers *if this was really the behavior they wanted to model.*

At the retail outlet, the young woman behind the front desk was texting and ignoring her coworker, who was asking for help. She then replied, "That's not my section." The customer, in the meantime, was noticing this and shaking his head in disapproval while having to wait. The task was taking the coworker about ten minutes but would have been cut in half if the two coworkers had worked together. *Did this organization really emphasize customer service?*

At the manufacturing plant, a new member of the team was sitting isolated, clearly wanting to engage, while the other three team members sat together joking, laughing, and ignoring him. *Did they really understand how productivity suffered from lack of engagement?*

Not working as a unit, not modeling the appropriate behavior, not understanding customer service, and not engaging as a team were all clear signs that these organizations needed additional assistance.

Later that evening, as I reflected on my day, I thought back to the seven attributes that continued to show up in my research. It was then that I realized what needed to be done to help these teams—and potentially, I hoped, teams all over the country. I envisioned a maze of challenges that encouraged team building. Each day, not just once a year, teams would work together to navigate them. The next day, I couldn't get the idea out of my head. While driving in the car with my husband, I told him about it, saying, "Wouldn't that be amazing?" The only problem was I didn't know what to call it. He turned to me and, as if it were the most obvious thing in the world, said, "aMAZEing Teams." Thus, the aMAZEing Team Building (ATB) Experience was born.

Over the next nine months, I worked to bring together a team of select individuals with two very distinct thought processes: an engineer with a Master of Engineering Management (MEM) degree and an organizational development professional with a Master of Science in Positive Organization Development & Change (MPOD) degree, both from Case Western Reserve University. Despite the obvious differences, these two thought processes came together in an incredible display of mental ability to make my vision of the aMAZEing Team Building Experience a reality.

The Seven Attributes

As I've said, our performance in the workplace today is in large part measured on an individual basis. What makes ATB unique is that it allows participants to think about performance *as an individual on a team*, rather than just as an individual. Today, aMAZEing Team Building is an indoor interactive team-building service based out of Cleveland, Ohio. Each week we guide teams from all different industries through a maze of challenges, each focusing on one of the seven attributes. Our expert facilitators guide, observe, and rate teams on their performance in each challenge, and teams leave with specific actionable items for improvement in each attribute.

As I put together the seven attributes, some people challenged me, saying that the meeting-management and behavior-management attributes should not be on the list. However, when I asked if they could achieve optimum productivity in their teams without those attributes, the answer was and continues to be "no."

Due to lack of prioritization, one of the biggest challenges teams face in applying these attributes is time. In today's fast-paced, do-more-with-fewer-resources, do-it-better-than-the-day-before culture, many important tasks get put on the back burner. If it's not something we are directly measured on, chances are we'll put off doing it until we have more time. And when will we have more time? If you're like most of the clients we see every day, you won't. This lack of prioritizing team building is a root cause of many of the issues we are called to help with every day. Without ensuring that our teams have the knowledge, skills, and tools to work together in a cohesive way, how can we expect them to be productive? We need to begin to focus on fixing the root cause of team challenges, and then we can begin to provide additional value, in less time, for our organizations.

Although some of these principles may seem like common sense to the seasoned professional, they are *not* commonly used. And until we intentionally put our focus on and prioritize the actions associated with these attributes, our teams will continue to operate only somewhere around that 70 percent level.

So, take a journey with us and find out how you can empower yourself and your teams to become more cohesive, productive, and resilient.

Trust

A team must believe in one another's ability, rely upon one another for support, and be confident that they can achieve more together than individually.

Author's Thoughts

I really didn't understand what people meant about trust in the workplace until I saw it firsthand. Several years ago, I had the opportunity to observe a manager over the course of several months. This manager consistently assigned work to a specific employee and not to another, because she knew that employee would get it done. Makes sense, right? I mean, why would you give work to someone you weren't sure could do the job right? But let's take a look at what happened. Toward the end of my time at the organization, I noticed two things: (1) The employee who continually received all the work burned out. She had been giving 110 percent for so long, she simply couldn't go on like that any longer. And (2) the employee who didn't receive any work lost motivation, and her skills declined. When I saw the outcome, it dawned on me that this was a form of trust that led to not one, but two, unhappy employees.

In another situation, I worked with someone who was extremely well versed at his job, consistently did what he said he would do, was very personable, and built great relationships with others. I was quite fond of him, but one day when I went to visit him, I ran into his team members. When we started talking about him, I was surprised to hear that they didn't like him. I started to ask questions and realized that while, yes, all the things I thought about this person were true, his decisions were continually made in his own best interest—not that of the team. Even if only one factor is questioned by others, you still lose their trust. It happens all the time inadvertently. We concentrate so much on our own teams, due to lack of time, more to do, and so on, that we forget to teach our teams to think of the impact on other people/departments when we make decisions. We tend to internally think of ourselves as divided, but our customers and clients think of the whole organization. The subdivisions that show up as departments are really just subteams. It is important to remember that we are all still one large team.

- -

Trust among Team Members

There must be confidence in team members to act with the best motivations and intentions of the team; there is no reason to be protective or careful around the group.

Why Do Teams Need Trust?

Trust is the "heart" of a highly functioning team. Without it, teamwork is impossible. Having trust within teams can increase efficiency, increase the team's willingness to take calculated risks, and even increase morale, which can also lead to an increase in productivity.

We've all heard it before—the old adage, *Actions speak louder than words*. And there is a reason we've all heard it before—it holds so much truth! We are influenced much more by actions than we are by words, which makes actions one of the primary building blocks of trust. Don't just talk the talk, but walk the walk. If we want someone to trust us, we have to demonstrate we are trustworthy vs. just saying we are. Let's take a look at some other behaviors that increase trust:

How much do you really trust your team?

- having **high self-awareness**
- **giving and offering trust** first
- leveraging trust-elevating **communication** techniques
- **putting forth your best effort** in the workplace
- **helping others** to succeed
- collaborating, cooperating, considering, and contributing
- **demonstrating competence** as a starting point

Now let's look at some behaviors that erode trust:

- **failing to keep promises**, agreements, and commitments
- serving yourself first, and others only when it is convenient
- **micromanaging** and **resisting delegation**
- demonstrating an **inconsistency** between words and behaviors
- **betraying** confidences, **gossiping**, and talking about others behind their backs
- choosing to not allow others to contribute or make decisions
- **failing to share** critical information with colleagues
- refusing to follow through on decisions agreed upon at team meetings

All of these actions lead to either increased or decreased trust, so it is critical that we take the time to evaluate our own actions on a continual basis. Let's break things down even further now and take a look at the components of trust, where many of these behaviors come into play.

- **Competence**—Your teammates believe in what you know.
- **Contractual**—Your teammates believe you will do what you promised.
- **Communication**—Your teammates believe what you say.
- **Social Interactions/Relationships**—Your teammates have a relationship and know you a level deeper than just the work.
- **Decision Making**—Your teammates know you consider and make decisions in the best interest of all stakeholders involved.

Competence—Your teammates believe in what you know. So, how do you know when others believe in what you know, and how can you increase your competence? First, they won't believe in what you know unless you are confident in your own knowledge. This means you must first know what you need to know and then consistently demonstrate your knowledge and expertise in your meetings, your work, and your interactions. You need to truly know your area of expertise and be knowledgeable based on your *level* and *job role*. No one is expecting a project manager to be an expert in the new IT system, but they do expect that person to know what they mean when they talk about "Waterfall," "Agile," or "critical paths," and for a senior project manager to be abreast of any new methods and tools in the PM world. So, how do you know what you need to know? This requires you to have a level of organizational and emotional awareness regarding what your organization values and what your strength development opportunities are; we call this the Credibility Quotient (CQ). Your EQ + your IQ = your CQ.

As industries, tools, techniques, and technology are always changing and evolving, this means that your competence level is always in need of continuous improvement, and you must take an intentional approach to maintaining it. So if this means you need to find a mentor, take additional courses to develop/continually improve your skills, subscribe to trade magazines, or simply put more time or effort into your job, then do it. No one wants to be thought of as a nice person but not competent in his or her role.

Contractual—Your teammates believe you will do what you promised. So, how do you get others to truly believe you will do what you say you will? Simple—do what you say and deliver on your promises. I heard someone say once, *Let your yes be yes and your no be no.* By consistently delivering on agreed-upon goals, tasks, and anything else, you will inspire confidence in others. But true contractual trust is made up of a little more than just consistent follow-through. It means that people understand what is expected of them, that roles and responsibilities are clear, and that employees collaborate freely, depend on each other, and deliver results. If I asked your coworkers right now if you followed through on your promises, what would they say? Are your words simply words, or do they hold value and meaning to others?

Communication—Your teammates believe what you say. Words followed by action. Notice a pattern? I can't emphasize this enough: If you say you are going to do something, then do it. But this aspect of trust takes a little different spin and also includes communicating the right information the right way. This means you have to understand who your audience is, the purpose of your communication, what information needs to be communicated, and the best method to do it, and think even further to how your audience will perceive/understand your message. If you do what you say you will and take into consideration these elements when communicating with others, their trust for you will increase.

Social Interactions/Relationships—Your teammates have a relationship and know you at a level deeper than just the work. This means creating connections through positive engagement. To do this, you must establish some point of connection. Maybe it's a shared alma mater, hobby, or your kids play in the same Little League; whatever it is, establishing a connection leads to feelings of similarity and relatability. If we can relate better to each other, our trust level automatically goes up. This requires us to have a certain level of cultural and personal awareness and ability to talk with others informally and continue the connection on an ongoing basis.

Decision Making—Your teammates know you consider and make decisions in the best interest of all stakeholders involved. We all know the type of leader who makes you feel like no matter what you say, it doesn't matter, because that leader is going to do whatever he or she wants anyhow. But this type of behavior does not foster trust; in fact, it does just the opposite. Before making decisions, good leaders must *consider* the impact of their actions/decisions through gathering feedback, including stakeholders in the process and being transparent. You must be willing to sometimes let go of your ego and consider things that the rest of group feels very strongly about. This will show others that you truly do value their ideas and insight and are willing to put your personal feelings aside for the good of the team.

Building a Culture of Trust

Now you might be thinking that this all sounds well and good, but how do you actually build a culture of trust in your organization? The answer is that building a culture of trust does not happen overnight. Building that kind of a culture takes time and dedication from many individuals. Too often we see a team work diligently to establish trust, but struggle because the rest of the organization does not operate the same way. To build a culture of trust, many individuals must take it upon themselves to do the things noted above, but also work to do the following:

- **Establish and maintain integrity.** This must be demonstrated by senior leadership.
- **Communicate vision and values**. Define where you're going and methods for getting there.
- **Consider all employees as equal partners.** Treat everyone with genuine respect.
- **Focus on shared, rather than personal, goals.** This is the essence of teamwork.
- And lastly, ***do what's right, regardless of personal risk!***

Team Discussion

Are you willing to do what's right all the time, regardless of personal risk?

Do you trust your team? *Why or why not?* Do others trust your team? *Why or why not?*

What does trust look like in your team? What would your team look like if you fully trusted one another?

Challenges

Individual Challenge: *Trust Bank Activity:* Write down any actions in the past or present that could impact the level of trust your team has for you. Write down both positive and negative actions *(those that lead to increased* trust and those that lead to decreased trust). What will you do to increase the positive actions and decrease the negative ones?

What area(s) of trust (competence, contractual, communication, social interactions/relationships, and decision making) do you feel you need to work on the most? What will you do to improve in those area(s)?

Team Challenge: Wipe the slate clean. Have an open and honest discussion to clear the air. Write your concerns about your team members on a slip of paper and have one person collect them. Commit to receiving the feedback from your team with an open mind and to working to make improvements. Schedule a team meeting to address the concerns as a group.

Appreciation

A team must have gratitude for one another and express their thankfulness sincerely and consistently.

Author's Thoughts

Many times I hear from clients, "I don't have a budget, so I can't appreciate people." What they don't understand is that it actually doesn't take very much to appreciate people. I do an exercise in class and ask people their preferred form of appreciation, and most of them say something other than money. Of course, we would all take more money if it was offered; we could all use some, even if you just donate it to charity. But most people really just want a simple thank you, a pat on the back, or somebody to help them out with a difficult task once in a while. Participation is the cost of everything. A lot of times we don't have time because we're trying to do too much. If everything is a priority, nothing is. So we don't take time to do many of the things that we're talking about as they relate to team attributes. Especially when it comes to appreciation. If we were to take just five minutes a day to stop and think about what someone has done to make our day easier and let him or her know that, I think it would save us hours each week. When people know they are appreciated, they work just a little bit harder, they put in a little bit more energy, and they expend a little bit more effort. They also think about reciprocation and paying back the very person who acknowledged them. It creates a workplace of high morale and an environment in which people feel motivated. That increased motivation leads to increased engagement, which leads to what? Increased productivity! And we all know the name of the game is productivity. We all want to do more. More doesn't mean more time; it could be more effort while we're there by putting forth our very best. Who wants to put their very best forward when they don't even feel as though they are appreciated for being there?

I know we sometimes use them interchangeably, but appreciation and recognition are actually very different. Recognition implies performance-based. People exceeded the goal, and they are rewarded for that. But appreciation simply refers to the fact that you acknowledge my value just for being in the workplace. I don't have to exceed any goal. It is basic human decency. I was once at a law firm, and the partners told me that one of their employees was upstairs packing up her office to leave the firm. One partner wanted to try to keep her, and the other was insistent that she was just wanting more rewards and money. By the time I got to her office, she had most of her belongings packed. I noticed a number of awards on the wall. I asked her why she wasn't taking them. I'll never forget what she told me. She said that they meant less to her than a simple thank you, which was all she wanted. She didn't want more money. She made way more than she ever thought she would. She said they were very generous to her with financial compensation, but no one seemed to care about giving her a simple "nice job," which would have gone much further than a bonus on her paycheck.

It's sad when we lose good employees when a simple thank you would have made them stay.

What Does Appreciation Look Like in Teams?

Appreciation shows itself in efforts made by management at an organization to acknowledge employees.

Types of Appreciation

With appreciation, it is the platinum rule vs. the golden rule. Appreciate people how they want to be appreciated vs. how you would like to be appreciated. Let's face it; we've all done it. At home, maybe we've taken a spouse to a crowded New Year's Eve party, when the spouse really would have preferred a nice cozy dinner alone with you. Or at work, you called one of your most introverted team members to the front of a large meeting to tell everyone how great a job he or she did, when your team member would have preferred a handshake in the privacy of his or her office.

Have you ever stopped to think of all the different ways people like to be appreciated?

Show your appreciation by **telling** someone.

Example: A manager saying thank you ... and genuinely meaning it.

Show your appreciation by **doing** something to help someone else.

Example: A colleague offering to stay late to help you complete a critical assignment even though it is not his or her responsibility.

Show your appreciation by providing someone with something that he or she **values**.

Example: While looking at your schedule, you realize you will be out of town for the next football game, and you are a season ticket holder. You decide to offer your tickets to one of your hardest working employees, who you know loves football and does not have the means to purchase his own tickets.

Show your appreciation by giving someone a **high five**.

Example: One of your team members just had a breakthrough idea in your team meeting, so you reach across the table and give her a high five.

Show your appreciation by giving someone your **undivided attention and time**.

Example: As a director, your time is limited. However, you continue to hear about how well one of your new employees is doing. One of your managers mentions that he overheard this person talking about how much she would love to meet you. You decide to make time to have lunch with her and express how happy you are to hear how well she is doing.

Why Is Appreciation Important?

With the numerous teams we are studying, we are finding that the number-one factor in job satisfaction is not the amount of pay, but whether or not the individual feels appreciated and valued for the work he or she does. When we interview past and present team members, those who leave or are contemplating leaving their jobs say they did or will do so because of lack of appreciation. So that means by changing this one small thing, you could potentially decrease turnover by as much as 64 percent in your organization! You may be asking why appreciation matters so much when we all get paid to do our jobs. Isn't that appreciation enough? No! A company maintains its most **valued assets not by compensation, but by appreciation**. Making sure that your team feels appreciated creates a more positive work climate, which means employees are more creative, productive, committed, and involved, ultimately reaching a higher level in accomplishing the organization's objectives. Bottom line, a person who feels appreciated will always do more than what is expected.

But before you go out high fiving and telling everyone how much you love them, there are a few things you need to remember when it comes to appreciating your colleagues. First, make sure that it is done *in the moment.* To be effective your appreciation needs to be timely, specific, descriptive, and measured. Second, it needs to be *in context.* Appreciation is more effective when given in the context of a larger goal or business-results-focused activity. Third, it needs to be *appropriate in volume/ scale.* It must match results, or it loses meaning. You are not going to announce to the whole organization that an employee did a great job on his or her last report, but you may announce to the whole organization if that employee just landed the biggest customer your organization has ever had. Fourth, it must be *authentic, not automatic.* Keep the "human touch"; don't get so used to dishing out appreciation that it is no longer genuine—people can tell, and it loses its meaning. One of the single **highest drivers of engagement** is whether or not workers **feel** their managers are **genuinely interested** in their well-being. And finally, it must be *tied to the employee's perception of value.* Remember all the awards the lawyer received that didn't mean anything to her?

Some simple suggestions to get you started:

- Know your coworkers' interests well. Don't know what they're into? Ask them!
- Praise something your coworker has done well.
- Say please and thank you *often.*

Sometimes all it takes is a simple thank you.

Team Discussion

What types of emotions do you feel when someone makes you feel appreciated?

Share a time when someone did something that really made you feel appreciated and what the outcome of that was.

What are some ways that your team can begin to build a culture of genuine appreciation both in your team and in your organization?

Challenges

Individual Challenge: Take some time to reflect on your own preferred style of appreciation. What is it? Then ask yourself if you are appreciating others based on the way you like to be appreciated *or* the way they prefer to be appreciated?

Team Challenge: In your next team meeting, have everyone guess their team members' preferred method of appreciation. Then go around the room and have everyone tell what theirs is. For the next four weeks, make it a point to do one thing each week to show your appreciation for someone on your team. After the four weeks are over, reflect on any changes either in atmosphere, behavior, or productivity that you noticed.

Communication

A team must be able to convey and receive messages in a constructive and healthy manner and use this information to create a sense of community through mutual understanding.

Author's Thoughts

When you were a kid, did you ever play the telephone game? By the end of the game, the message is usually so garbled and confused that it seems too far-fetched to believe this can actually happen in real life, right? However, you might be surprised at how often I see this in organizations. Oftentimes, a lot of people are talking, but no communication is really taking place because we are all too busy waiting for our turn to talk that we forget to listen. Listening is about attunement and really checking in to the other person, something that we as a society are not great at. You can walk in with your position or topic, but true listening means that you consider what the other person has to say, and as a result of the conversation, you may actually change your view or hybridize the two views. When someone feels he or she is not really being heard, conflict ensues.

One of the top reasons for lack of engagement or poor organizational scores on employee evaluations is due to problems with communication. But what does that mean? Communication is too big of a problem to solve on its own. It has to be broken into different components. I always start by asking people what component of communication is really causing the problem, and more often than not, they don't know. We can't solve for something we don't know. The truth is that if we can't get to the root cause of the communication problem, people are going to continue to talk with no one really listening. To communicate effectively, we have to be intentional and think of the individual components each and every time we open our mouths or type words on a screen.

Communication in Teams

Communication is the ability to choose the right words, listen with your mind, and convey a clear, concise message.

Why Is Effective Communication Important?

Have you ever been frustrated because someone didn't listen to you or completely misunderstood what you were trying to say? If the answer is yes *(which I'm sure it is!)*, then you know how detrimental ineffective communication can be to relationships and to an organization. Effective communication conveys direction within the organization and creates an inclusive environment. It enables the team to create and build a more trusting environment and engage in meaningful dialogue. It saves teams time when making decisions and solving conflicts, thereby increasing effectiveness throughout the entire organization. Really, communication has a huge impact on how successful we as a team are with the other attributes. Without nailing this one, it is very difficult to achieve success in the others.

Elements of Effective Communication

Oftentimes we get frustrated when our attempts to communicate fail, but have you ever stopped to think that maybe the problem isn't with others ... that the problem may be with you? All communication has both a sender and a receiver. We must always remember to distinguish the message from the messenger. Sometimes because we don't like the messenger, we can't hear the message. And sometimes because we don't like the message, we can't hear the messenger.

Take a look at the indicators of both effective and ineffective communication below and ask yourself which ones best describe you.

| 1) You only share information when asked. | 2) You share as little communication as possible. | 3) You have difficulty listening to others. |

or

| 1) You share information openly and honestly. | 2) You keep everyone informed of all relevant updates. | 3) You seek to understand and clarify. |

If you relate most to the first set of indicators, you may want to pay particular attention to this chapter. Let's take a look at some basic elements of communication that can have a big impact on how effective our communication truly is.

Volume: *The **volume** of communication is determined by how much you say at one time.*

How do you know you are communicating with the right level of detail? Ever sent an important e-mail, and no one read it because it was "too long"? Frustrating, right? Well, here are some tips to ensure you are not putting your colleagues on information overload:

- Spend less time on gaining/providing information that is **nice to know** and more time on information that others **need to know.**
- Focus on the **quality of information**, rather than the quantity. *A short, concise e-mail can oftentimes be more valuable than a long e-mail.*
- **Be direct** in what you ask people, so that they can provide short, precise answers.
- **Avoid multitasking**. Keep your mind focused on one topic at a time.

Content: *The content of communication is determined by what you say.*

Have you ever listened to someone talk, and it was so convoluted that you had no idea what the person was trying to say so you just stopped listening? Here are some tips to make sure that person isn't you. Just remember the **6 Cs**.

1. **Clear**—Make sure your message is clear.
2. **Compelling**—Make sure your message will resonate with your audience (we'll address this in detail later on). If the message content resonates and connects on some level with the receiver, it will be most effective.
3. **Consistent**—Make sure if you send more than one message or if you have more than one sender that your message is consistent.
4. **Correct**—Make sure you have your facts straight before communicating anything.
5. **Coherent**—Be well organized. No one will understand your message if you are jumping from one thought to the next without a logical flow.
6. **Concise**—Describe in just enough detail to obtain understanding from the receiver.

Frequency: *The frequency of communication is determined by how often you say something.*

Have you ever received the same e-mails so many times that pretty soon you just delete them without a second glance? Or have you ever received critical information about a change several months before it was going to take place and then never heard about it again? Communicating at the right frequency is required for the proper functioning of an organization. When trying to determine the right frequency of your message, consider these things:

- *How often are you repeating yourself?*
- *How often are you hearing the same discussions?*
- *Is this message critical for the receiver or just nice to know?*

Several years ago I had a client who was spending more than two hours each day reading through e-mails he was copied on. Ninety percent of the e-mails only contained nice-to-know information that people copied him on because of his position. He didn't really need the information, but it was impossible to know which of the e-mails he received contained information he really did need to know, so he had to read through them all. He was wasting over two hours of his time each day on a task that added no value. It wasn't until he came up with a new e-mail communication policy that he was able to take back his time.

Delivery of the Message: *Delivery of the message* is the way in which you determine how and to whom to send a message.

In today's fast-paced business world, we get busy and forget to think through the content of our message and choose the most effective and efficient communication tool to deliver it. Before delivering your next message, ask yourself the following:

- What is the best **mechanism** for communicating my message (e-mail, in person, one-to-one, by phone, in a meeting, etc.)?
- Am I using the right **approach** for my message (tone, intent, attitude, volume, etc.)?
- Is this the right **timing** for my message (when)?
- Do I know my **audience** and their **needs** (who)?

Identify with Your Audience

Now let's jump back to a topic that we brought up earlier—making sure that your message is compelling. What makes a message compelling to some is not what will make it compelling for others. So how do you know what to say? You start by understanding what's important to your audience. Sometimes you might have to modify how you communicate a specific message in order to best resonate with your specific audiences.

Here is a simple technique to try. First, draw a table with two columns. Write "Audience" in the top left and "Area of Focus/Concern" in the top right. Then underneath list all of your different audiences and what you think their primary concerns are. Then you will know what you need to effectively communicate to that particular audience.

How well do you know your audience?

Audience	Area of Focus/Concern
Audience 1	
Audience 2, etc.	

Nonverbal Communication

Have you ever stopped to consider what your behaviors, attitudes, and actions are really communicating?

Our body language has a great impact on how we communicate and can often reflect how we are feeling on the inside.

Body language includes:

body movements and gestures (legs, arms, hands, head, and torso) • Posture • Muscle tension • Eye contact • Skin coloring (flushed red) • breathing rate and perspiration

The most noticeable type of body language is the **gesture.** This can be a movement or position of the hand, arm, body, head, or face that is expressive of an idea, opinion, emotion, and so on. It is extremely important to recognize that body language and gestures may vary between individuals and between different cultures and nationalities, so if you are working with other ethnicities or traveling to another country, it would be wise to do a little research into their culture to ensure you don't accidentally do something to offend them.

Oftentimes we don't even realize we are doing something that may be distracting others from our message. A great exercise to help you become a better nonverbal communicator is to record yourself and then watch and critique your nonverbal cues. For something that makes up 55 percent of your message, it is well worth your time to do this.

On the other hand, it is also essential to verify and confirm the signals that you are reading in someone else by further communicating and seeking to understand his or her point of view.

Creating a Culture of Shared Communication

Let's face it: we could do everything right to ensure we are communicating effectively, and our message may still not be received the way we would like. The fact is that our work environment affects our communication and whether it is well received. So how do we build a culture of shared communication? Well, it doesn't happen overnight, but here are some tips to get you started:

- **Open communication:** This starts at the top. Make sure that your colleagues and staff feel comfortable and that there is consistent transparency in your messages.
- **Employee involvement:** Get everyone involved by ensuring your messages identify with their needs.
- **Shared goals:** Make sure that everyone understands and is committed to the organization's goals.
- **Collaboration between departments:** Break down invisible silos between departments, so the message is heard regardless of the messenger.

Team Discussion

What are the biggest communication challenges your team/organization faces?

What can your team do to address those challenges?

In what ways can your team help create a culture of shared communication?

Challenges

Individual Challenge: Before you send out your next e-mail or get the team together for a meeting, go through the communication factors and make sure that you are communicating as effectively as you can. List the ways you effectively communicate and list the areas where you need improvement.

Team Challenge: Make a list of the most common messages that need to be communicated among your team. Then determine the most effective ways to make sure that they are heard and understood. Go through the communication factors and make a table for each message that looks like this:

Message Type	Audience	Volume	Content	Frequency	Delivery Mechanism	Timing

Behavior Management

A team must govern themselves in a way that increases engagement, trust, and collaboration among the members.

We judge ourselves by our intentions; others judge us by our behavior. We don't see our behavior; others don't see our intentions. —Author Unknown

Author's Thoughts

My father once told me to act as though cameras are always on you and treat people in a way that you never have to apologize. That thought has always stuck with me to beware of my behavior at all times and treat people with respect, despite how they may act. In other words, be the professional in the situation. And today, the cameras really might be on us. We are human and we make mistakes that we might have to apologize for, but some people have a repeat pattern of having to apologize rather than regulating their unproductive or disruptive behavior.

The other thing we have to remember is that just because we have the right to do something doesn't make it right to do so. We have the right to say a lot of things that are protected by our First Amendment, but before we speak, we need to stop and let our words pass through four gates: Is it true? Is it appropriate? Is it necessary? And is it kind? These are words I heard from my mother on a regular basis. If we simply used this as our test for communication, we would prevent a significant number of behavior-related communication issues.

It is very difficult for us to have responsibility for others when we can't govern ourselves. We talk about leadership, but leadership starts with intent. So, stay with me here. Our **thoughts** drive our **intent**, which shows up in our **behavior**, which then dictates our **leadership traits**, and if this action is repeated, it forms our **leadership style**, which then becomes our **image or reputation**. So the first thing is to really think about the intentions behind our words and actions. Behavior plays such a critical part of human interaction, but surprisingly we stop talking about it on a regular basis after elementary school.

What Is Behavior Management?

Behavior management requires awareness of your emotions to stay flexible and direct your behavior positively. It involves managing your emotional reactions to situations and people (think performance, actions, deeds, activities, manners, and conduct).

Why Is Behavior Management Important?

Have you ever wished you could go back in time and change the way you responded to a situation at work? Maybe it was an emotionally charged conversation, and you didn't even know you felt so strongly until you were in the middle of it. If you are unable to control how you react to situations at work, it is not likely that you will be climbing the corporate ladder anytime soon. But in order to *control* our behavior, we must first be aware of the emotions that drive it. It is essential that we don't allow our performance to be affected by frustration or anger. But how do we do that? Well, it starts with self-awareness, which means being able to recognize the emotions that we experience, understand the feelings associated with the emotions, and understand what we think and do as a result. So, self-awareness and self-regulation are both key to managing our behavior.

How often do you let your emotions control you?

Don't think you have a good handle on these competencies? Well, the good news is that self-awareness and self-regulation can be developed, but it takes intentional focus and continual work. The results however, will be well worth it.

Self-Regulation—What's Really Happening Inside Your Brain

Once you are aware of your emotions, you need to know what is really going on inside your brain that will allow you to regulate and change your behaviors. Ever hear about something called neuroplasticity? I hadn't until I started my research. You see, the brain is inherently dynamic and changeable, a characteristic called *neuroplasticity*. So what does this mean for behavior? It means that anytime you do something, you're more likely to do it again. Whether our actions and behaviors are intentional or unintentional, they get woven into the neural structures of our brain and develop our patterns of thinking and behavior. As this information is reinforced through repetition, it becomes wired in our brain and solidifies our thoughts and actions. In essence, it becomes who you are, and hence your image and reputation. Not liking the memory of your last interaction with an annoying coworker? Well, there's good news! If our mind is truly dynamic, which neuroplasticity says it is, we can alter our wiring to develop new patterns of thinking and behavior. But this is only accomplished through deliberate practice. Also, look for a coach or mentor to give you feedback and hold you accountable. It is also important to be optimistic. You didn't build your old pathways overnight, so it will take time to build new ones. And like anything else, practice can be hard work. But by keeping a positive mental attitude, you'll be more likely to stick with it and replace those existing neural pathways with new pathways and behaviors.

The Results

By intentionally focusing on managing unproductive/disruptive behaviors, you are much more likely to:

- reach your desired performance through appropriate actions,
- generate performance that helps establish your credibility with your superiors and peers,
- meet others at their individual level of need by being able to adapt your personal style and approach to meet the situation, and
- manage others to achieve.

So, don't let your emotions hold you back from achieving success in both your work and personal life. Remember, *the evidence of learning is changed behavior.*

*Our **thoughts** drive our **intent**,*
*Which shows up in our **behavior**,*
Which then dictates our
leadership traits.
Then through repetition it forms
*our **leadership style**,*
Which then becomes our
image or reputation.

Team Discussion

Think of a time when you let your emotions control you.

- Were you aware of your emotions at the time?
- What was the consequence of those unregulated emotional reactions?
- How did it impact your team?
- What can you do to practice changing your behavioral patterns?

Challenges

Individual Challenge: Using the table below, rate your level of self-awareness and self-regulation. Spend some time recognizing aspects of yourself that you need to intentionally develop/strengthen and identify ways you can do that.

Emotional Intelligence Attributes		Rating Never Always	Strength Y N	Actions to Improve
Self-Awareness	Do you understand your own emotions, strengths, weaknesses, drives, values, and goals?	1 2 3 4 5		
	Do you recognize their impact on others?	1 2 3 4 5		
Self-Regulation	Are you able to control or redirect your disruptive emotions and impulses?	1 2 3 4 5		
	Are you able to adapt to changing circumstances?	1 2 3 4 5		

Team Challenge: Identify any negative patterns in behavior that you must overcome in order to operate more effectively as a team and discuss ways to improve. Write these down and spend five minutes at the start of each team meeting discussing your team's progress.

Meeting Management

A team must use their meetings to achieve productive outcomes.

Author's Thoughts

I often ask people if they like meetings. The answer is usually no. I tell them not liking a meeting is the same as not liking a hammer. A hammer is just a tool. Why would you dislike a tool? Well, if you're using a hammer to screw in a lightbulb, you really didn't need the hammer in the first place. The point is, many of us don't dislike the tool, but we dislike the way we misuse it in our workplace.

Meetings are actually one of the best tools a team can use to resolve issues, to brainstorm, to plan, to update one another on relevant information, to discuss ways to improve processes, to problem solve, to generate ideas, and the list goes on.

I actually stopped doing agendas a long time ago, even for public organizations that I work with where agendas are required. An agenda is just a list of topics. We could talk all day about a list of topics and never resolve or solve anything. I take it a step further and ask, *what are the expected outcomes for each of those topics?* Each meeting should have expected outcomes. For any meeting, if you can't answer why, what, who, when, where, and how, you should really rethink whether you should be having the meeting at all.

I actually went through my calendar and eliminated every meeting that was not productive by those standards. I freed up a day and a half each week. If organizations would just go through this exercise, they would gain back significant time to concentrate on the other team attributes.

Much of our time is spent in meetings, yet we do so poorly executing them. I was talking to a senior executive, and he said he really wanted to concentrate on meeting management. I asked if that was too far in the weeds for him. He said absolutely not. He said that if any employee in his organization took money from the safe, he or she would be fired, and if any employee stole product, she or he would be fired. But yet we call meetings every day for a great majority of the day and waste away company money in terms of salary time, and we do nothing about it.

I no longer see just people in meetings. I see salaries and brains. There is way too much money there to walk in not knowing why you are there and walk out not having solved anything. There is way too much talent and brainpower to not prevent problems and resolve critical issues.

Meeting management is an area we really should concentrate on more. Researchers that I consulted with questioned whether or not meeting management should be a team attribute ... I completely and strongly insisted it should. We spend more time in meetings than just about anything else we do. Yet meeting management is the most poorly used tool I can think of in the workplace. If we use it so much, why are we not excellent at it?

What Is Meeting Management?

> *A meeting is simply a collaborative gathering convened*
> *for the purpose of achieving a common goal, and good*
> *meeting management leads to productive outcomes.*

Why Is Effective Meeting Management Important?

Over half of the nearly twenty CEOs that we have worked with in the course of our teamwork feel their organization is not getting maximum ROI from their meetings and events. Over 40 percent of the nearly twenty-five CFOs that we have worked with are not satisfied with their company's spend management related to travel and meetings.

Being able to effectively manage meetings is critical to keeping the organization on track and providing teams with the forum they need to make decisions and obtain results.

Calculating the True Cost of Your Meetings

Have you ever sat down to calculate how much your meetings actually cost? We're not talking about meeting space or bottled water, but human capital—salaries. For the last meeting you attended, try to calculate the cost following the steps below. Use estimations for employees whose salaries you don't know.

- Make a list of **who** was there.
- Estimate the **pay rate per hour** of each individual.
- Write down how **long** the meeting was.
- Make a list of what was **accomplished (value added)** from the meeting.

Most Common Meeting Challenges

Let's face it, some of the most common challenges we face in meetings are the easiest to solve. So why aren't we solving them? The answer is simple: time and prioritization. We are faced with trying to do more and more with fewer resources, so taking the time to properly prepare for meetings often falls to the bottom of our to-do list. But by spending our time up front, we will actually save time in the long run by not wasting our time in lengthy unproductive meetings.

Do these faces look familiar?

Do any of these meeting troubles sound familiar?

- starting late
- running long
- going off topic
- not being productive
- dealing with disruptive behaviors
- not having meeting outcomes
- not having an agenda or having a poorly prepared agenda
- not distributing the agenda ahead of time

So what can we do about these common challenges that plague our meetings? To start, we can follow these simple steps to plan for an effective meeting.

1. Determine the purpose/goal and desired outcomes.
2. Determine the type of the meeting/the form of the meeting.
3. Draw up a draft agenda and design the group processes to attain the necessary results.
4. Establish who needs to attend.
5. Determine the time/location.
6. Share the agenda with potential attendees, changing it as necessary. Ensure everyone gets fully briefed for the meeting and that everyone knows the purpose and potential consequences of the meeting.

Meeting Management Planning Grid

Meeting Type/ Topic	Desired Outcome	Attendee(s)	Role in Meeting	Prework (Assignment or Pre-Meeting)	Strategy or Tool	Actual Outcome and Actions

By simply taking the time to plan a better meeting, we can eliminate most of the common meeting challenges on our list.

Disruptive Behaviors

Now let's talk about the elephant in the room. You can do all the planning and preparation in the world, but there are always going to be those people who can make meetings difficult. Many times it is inadvertent, but unless properly addressed, these behaviors will take over your meeting. Say hello to ...

- **The arguers:** Emotional and combative, the arguers tend to take a firm stand on what they want and can be dismissive of others in the group. They can cause conflict by making group members feel abused, resentful, and unsatisfied with the process.
- **The quibblers:** They tend to be distracted by trivial issues and objections, and they evade the importance of issues through criticism for petty reasons.
- **The talkers:** The talkers feel they are contributing to the group by sharing their personal insights in order to seek recognition. Their efforts can be distracting and a nuisance for fellow group members.
- **The know-it-alls:** These attention seekers are driven by the need to feel validated. They may be knowledgeable in the subject at hand and can be overly eager to share their knowledge. They have a tendency to be overly talkative.
- **The happy wanderers:** They tend to lose focus on the task at hand. They may misunderstand topics and comment incorrectly due to lack of attention. They also may not be able to express their thoughts articulately.
- **The would-be leaders:** These attendees can be highly assertive and will lean toward a collaborative style to try to meet the needs

of everyone involved. They can effectively cooperate with others and recognize their value.

- **The shy introverts:** These attendees recognize conflict but avoid confrontation. They are generally quiet and withdrawn, with disinterest in conflict. They will compromise their needs in order to avoid conflict.

Recognize anyone you know? Maybe even yourself? Take a look below for some quick high-level strategies for dealing with these behaviors.

*Strategies for the **Arguer***

Remain neutral and do not get drawn into the argument. It is important to move on from the problematic topic. Allow others to give their opinion about the issue, but keep the focus on the agenda. Take time to speak with the argumentative party in order to get more insight. Always keep control of the room. Remind the group that you are all on the same team and would like to work together as a solid unit. Defuse the situation by assuring the arguer that you are willing to speak with him or her further at the completion of the meeting.

*Strategies for the **Quibbler***

Acknowledge the participant's contribution, but bring focus back to the relevant points of the agenda. Continually acknowledge interest and refocus on the agenda. Display a sense of urgency in meetings. Make continual efforts to emphasize the time. Oftentimes the quibbler will comment because he or she may feel as though there is enough time to deviate from the topic.

*Strategies for the **Talker***

Recognize the talker's contribution but refocus on the pertinent issues, keeping with the agenda. The talker is similar to the quibbler. Although content may be relevant to the topic at hand, he or she may want to take the opportunity to vent. Remember to convey a sense of urgency in meetings. Assure talkers that they may hold their story to share until the end of the meeting or a lunch break. If the subject is truly important to them, they will accept your offer and discuss it later.

Strategies for the **Know-It-All**

> Ask the participant challenging questions and keep the focus on the relevant issues of the topic. Allow the group dynamic to manage the individual as much as possible. Usually the know-it-all will try to answer or comment on every question. Remember that there are others in the meeting. Take advantage of every attempt to involve others in the room. Say things like: "Joe, I know you know the answer, but I would like to hear from Susan" (possibly the shy introvert).

Strategies for the **Happy Wanderer**

> Avoid embarrassment by acknowledging the point he or she may be trying to make and bring the wanderer back around to the topic at hand. Repeat relevant points when necessary to keep the participants on track. Be sure to try to get a sense of their point of view when they answer; they may be on the right track and need some guidance. Ask questions like: "How is this related to the current agenda/conversation?" or "How does this help us accomplish our meeting goal today?" and then actually hold them accountable to answer.

Strategies for the **Would-Be Leader**

> Encourage the participant's collaborative approach and help guide the situation in order to reach the best solution possible. Make consistent efforts to ask the would-be leader to provide assistance in facilitating the meeting. If you conduct any group activities, volunteer them as a default team leader.

Strategies for the **Shy Introvert**

> Understand that the participant may feel insecure, bored, or disinterested. Draw out interest by seeking his or her opinion. Get others in the group involved. And show sincere recognition for his or her participation. Open conversations that involve the entire room. Everyone should get a turn to answer or comment. Ask questions like, "Dan, what do you think about that? or "Jill, what's your opinion on …?"

The bottom line with these behaviors is that it is important to take the time to identify who these people may be in your meetings and what the appropriate strategies are for dealing with them ahead of time. Doing this will go a long way toward making your meetings more productive.

And finally, remember, if you fail to plan, then you *plan to fail.*

Team Discussion

Typically, how productive are your team meetings?

What challenges does your team/organization most commonly face in meetings? What can you do to address and fix them?

What types of behaviors typically show up in your meetings and how are they handled?

Challenges

Individual Challenge: Identify one thing that you can contribute/control to help make your team meetings more efficient and effective. Are you guilty of displaying one or more of the disruptive behaviors? If yes, what will you do to change that?

Team Challenge: For all your meetings this year, keep a detailed record of the value-added outcomes from each meeting. Then use the cost-of-meetings formula for estimating the cost for each meeting. If this was your money, was it worth it?

Problem Solving and Decision Making

A team must solve problems in a way that makes the solution sustainable and makes decisions in the best interest of all stakeholders.

Author's Thoughts

We're back to lack of prioritization again. Many times we say we don't have time to prevent, but we always seem to find time to react. The fact is, we work the way we are rewarded, and a lot of the time we are rewarded for fighting fires. For example, running to a customer's aid to fix a defect. I get that, but if we had been planning ahead, it probably wouldn't have happened in the first place. We are rewarded for bad behavior instead of being rewarded for preventing issues from happening. Because of this, we are in reactive mode most of the time at work. We're running so hard and so fast that we forget to stop and plan. And planning is a key to basic problem solving.

Actually it's funny—we would have a problem-solving problem prevented! I always say, you either pay now or pay later. We don't spend any up-front time to prevent issues, but I always wonder where we find the time to fight fires every day. That's got to be way more time than a few hours upfront preventing them from happening in the first place.

I was at a customer's facility once, and they were giving out an award for a guy who solved a really big outage. They gave him a fifty-dollar gift certificate. I remember being at that same client's a few weeks earlier, and someone was talking about the trend and it was looking as though the outage was going to happen. He wanted to talk about ways to prevent it, but no one had time for the meeting. I didn't want to put a damper on the special occasion, but I had to ask, "If he gets $50 for putting out the fire, should you pay the guy who tried to prevent it $100?"

Problem Solving and Decision Making

> *Problem Solving*—Analyzing challenges in a systematic way, leading to effective solutions that solve the root cause of problems.

> *Decision Making*—The cognitive process resulting in a final choice among several alternative possibilities.

Why Are Problem Solving and Decision Making So Important?

In this section we're really talking about two separate concepts, each with a unique set of challenges. Problem solving is about creating new solutions or new ways to work that lead to increased productivity. Oftentimes, even if teams successfully come up with some great ideas to solve their problems, they get stuck here. That's where decision making comes in. The challenge then becomes working together as a team to select the best option.

Just think, if we were really good at solving problems and making decisions, how much time, effort, and resources could we save our organizations over the course of a month, a year, or even ten years? So why are we spending so much time putting Band-Aids on to stop the bleeding and settling for less than optimal solutions?

Effective problem solving and decision making enable teams to:

- understand problems,
- focus on measures that drive strategy,
- understand root causes, and
- use facts and data to make decisions.

Former Secretary of State for President Eisenhower, John Foster Dulles, once said, *"The measure of success is not whether you have a tough problem to deal with, but whether it is the same problem you had last year."* Based on that criterion, how successful are you? Are you still dealing with some of the same problems you dealt with last year? If the answer is yes, do you know why?

Keys to Problem Solving and Decision Making

Problems are an inescapable part of the business world. We tend to jump into problem-solving mode at the first sign of trouble, thinking that if we *react* quickly enough, the problem's impact will be lessened. Now in some cases, this may in fact be true. However, what happens if we solve for the wrong problem because we jumped in too quickly? Then what did we really accomplish? We said earlier that planning is a key to problem solving. Teams in general need to develop a rhythm for problem solving that is specific to their organization. This rhythm should set the precedent that it is okay to spend more time up front defining and analyzing the problem vs. on the back end trying to come up with solutions to fix it.

Being able to critically think about and analyze a problem is essential to effective problem solving. The necessary skills include observation, interpretation, analysis, inference, evaluation, explanation, and metacognition. These skills enable individuals and teams to:

- recognize and correctly identify true problems, not just their symptoms
- drill down to the root cause of problems
- collect and analyze all relevant data/information to draw accurate conclusions
- understand and be able to communicate with accuracy, clarity, and discernment
- recognize and make connections between past experiences and the problem at hand
- make accurate judgments and utilize the appropriate strategies and tools to best solve the problem

Take a moment now to think about which of these areas highlight your strengths and which areas you may need to work on developing.

Now, let's take a look at a problem-solving methodology that can help your teams ensure they find effective and sustainable solutions to problems.

The Problem-Solving Methodology

There are five steps to this problem-solving methodology:

1) Step back to see the problem/issue differently.
2) Get to the root cause through questioning.
3) Use data/facts to make decisions.
4) Plan the course of action.
5) Sustain the improvement.

Step Back to See the Problem/Issue Differently

What do we do when we hear there's a problem? Right away, we want to solve it, so we begin brainstorming ideas of how to do that. At first this doesn't seem so bad; I mean, we all want the problem fixed, right? But by doing this, we realize later on that the problem we thought we were dealing with wasn't as big or as small, as complicated or as simple, as we originally thought. Remember, it goes back to planning.

One of the greatest minds of our time, Albert Einstein, said, *"If I had an hour to solve a problem, I'd spend fifty-five minutes thinking about the problem and five minutes thinking about solutions."* If Albert Einstein said he would rather spend the majority of his time thinking about the problem than jump to identify potential solutions, why do we think we know better?

We should look at the problem from a different angle or perspective. Approach it not just from your history, but from the stand point of someone in a different functional area, with a different background or history, and/or with different end goals to see what you might be missing by just considering your perspective. Stepping back also means looking at the extremes and all possibilities in the middle of these extremes. One way we can train ourselves to take a step back is to do something we learned in elementary school. Answer the basic questions first: who, what, where, when, why, and how. They seem simple, but if you *miss one*, you are in trouble. If you answer them *all*, you win big.

Where do you spend your time? Preventing problems or putting out fires?

Get to the Root Cause through Questioning

There are many root-cause analysis tools out there, and for the most part, they are really simple. Think Y = f(x), fishbone diagrams, and five whys. All these will help you stop the bleeding at the source vs. just putting a Band-Aid on the problem.

Not familiar with these tools? Here's a quick overview:

Y = f(x): A tool that allows teams to list and drill down process variables (causes) that may have a critical impact on the output (effect). Start by listing your problem (the Y), and then list out all the possible variables that could contribute to the problem (the Xs).

Inefficient Sales Process = $f($ level of sales team expertise, technology, training, sales materials $)$

Fishbone, Cause and Effect, or Ishikawa Diagrams: Brainstorming tools that help define and display major causes, subcauses, and root causes that influence a process. These tools allow teams to visualize the potential relationship among causes that may be creating problems or defects.

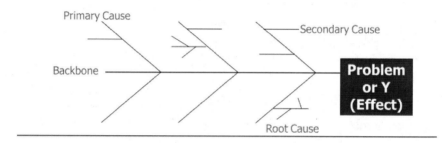

The Five-Why Method: A tool designed to address an issue by defining its root cause through asking the question "Why?" Five is an arbitrary number, as long as the root cause is identified.

Example of when a key piece of equipment has failed:

- Why did the equipment fail? *Because the circuit board burned out.*
- Why did the circuit board burn out? *Because it overheated.*
- Why did it overheat? *Because it wasn't getting enough air.*
- Why was it not getting enough air? *Because the filter wasn't changed.*
- Why was the filter not changed? *Because there was no preventive maintenance schedule to do so.*

Once you have identified that root cause, don't stop there. Let's think of it from a customer perspective ... what value are you adding for the customer, and how will you know if you've been successful?

Take a look at the following example: *Problem: A device does not have a way to indicate when it has been exposed to water.*

- *Customer Request:* A water color indicator that turns blue

- *Real Need:* A way to indicate that the device has been exposed to water
- *Value-Added Solution:* Turns pink (much easier to do chemically and costs $15 less per device x 2.5 million devices /year)
- *Measurable Outcome:* Money saved per device

Use Data/Facts to Make Decisions

We often rely on our gut to make decisions, using words such as "I think" and "I feel." Now don't misunderstand; there is a place for your gut, especially when you have past experience in the area in question, but when you are trying to get a group of people to make a decision on a course of action, data and facts go much further. What happens, though, when you have relied on facts and data and even implored your gut, and your team still is at an impasse? Half of your team thinks solution A is the right choice, whereas the other thinks that solution B is the way to go. How do you get them all to agree? And do you really need them to?

The Difference between Agreement and Alignment

On the surface, the difference between these two words may not be clear. After all, aren't *alignment* and *agreement* essentially the same thing? If your employees are in *alignment,* surely they must be in *agreement*! Well, not so fast.

If you're going to have a team that can make decisions for the good of the organization, you're going to need to know exactly what that difference is.

Definition of **Alignment**: Everyone is heading in the same direction and knows what they are heading to.

Definition of **Agreement**: Everyone thinks that where they are heading and what they are heading to is the *right thing*.

To summarize, a team can be *aligned* with a decision even though some members may not agree that it is the best decision. However, they are willing to *align* themselves in support of it for the good of the team and the organization.

So the next time your team is at an impasse, remember, you don't always need 100 percent agreement—just ensure alignment and move on.

The Most Common Decision-Making Challenges

It is important to have clear roles and expectations up front; otherwise, by the time you are able to make a decision, the competition may have already passed you up or an opportunity has been lost. A simple tool that can help reduce that ambiguity is called a RAPID matrix (a slightly different take on the popular RACI matrix, which we'll talk about later).

The letters stand for the primary roles in any decision-making process: recommend, agree, perform, input, and decide.

- The people who *recommend* a course of action are responsible for proposing potential solutions/alternatives.
- The people who *agree* to a recommendation are those who need to sign off on it before it can move forward.
- The people who will *perform* the decision ensure that the decision is implemented promptly and effectively.
- People with *input* responsibilities are consulted about the recommendation.
- Eventually, one person will *decide*. The decision maker is the single point of accountability who has the authority to commit the organization to act on it.

Now this tool won't solve all your problems, but clearly identifying and agreeing on these roles and responsibilities up front will go a long way to helping you to ensure your decisions are made in a timely and effective manner.

Another common challenge with decision making that we previously mentioned is getting those with the decision-making power to intentionally focus not just on the decision's impact on themselves, but taking into consideration how the team and other stakeholders are impacted as well. Many times this is not done intentionally, we just get so busy trying to get things done that we forget to take the time to shift our focus from the *"What's in It for Me"* (WIIFM) mentality to thinking about how it impacts everyone else. A simple way to help shift that focus is to conduct a stakeholder analysis. Simply list out all the different groups that would be impacted by the decision and then determine their level of impact (high, medium, low). Sometimes a decision impacts many more people/groups than originally anticipated, and it isn't until going through this exercise that the full breadth of the decision's reach and impact is understood. This will also help during implementation of any actions associated with the decision, because now you'll know whom you need to communicate with.

Plan the Course of Action

And we're back to planning. This time we are planning the course of action or resolution resulting from our root cause and data gathering analyses. The key to planning is taking the time to do it. Often times we are running from meeting to meeting and not taking time to really think though the steps needed to solve the problem based on the facts. It requires that we have subject matter experts and those who use and those who manage the process involved in the planning. We need an organized and systematic way to map out the required actions to get to resolution. At this step, there should be a clear and visual documentation of the process required to solve the problem, along with the decision points that must be considered.

Sustain the Improvement

Be sure that your plan includes ways to sustain your improvement. We often get so excited once we have finally decided on and implemented our solution that we forget this last step. Two factors that play a major role in this are monitoring and accountability. *Monitoring* requires operators/ engineers, managers, and so on to follow designated control methods to guarantee product/service quality throughout the system. We often make this more complicated than it needs to be. It could be as simple as identifying a few key performance indicators (KPIs) and tracking them every few months. *Accountability*, on the other hand, deals more with the people side of things and can be a bit trickier. But if done right, it will prevent the need for repeatedly solving the same problems. Be sure your people know their roles and your expectations up front. Remember, people work the way they're measured, so be sure to tie important measures into performance reviews if you can. Another simple tool you can use is called a RACI matrix. This tool identifies who is **r**esponsible, **a**ccountable, **c**onsulted, and **i**nformed for any given task and eliminates the guesswork for employees.

- **Responsible:** Those who do the work to achieve the task. There is at least one role where someone is responsible, although others can be delegated to assist in the work required.
- **Accountable:** The one ultimately answerable for the correct and thorough completion of the deliverable or task, and the one

who delegates the work to those responsible. In other words, an accountable must sign off (approve) work that a responsible party provides. There must be only one accountable specified for each task or deliverable.

- **Consulted:** Those whose opinions are sought, typically subject-matter experts, and with whom there is two-way communication.
- **Informed:** Those who are kept up-to-date on progress, often only on completion of the task or deliverable, and with whom there is just one-way communication.

And so, leading into our next section, "Creativity and Ideation," I'll leave you with this quote by founder and CEO of Selling Power, Inc., Gerhard Gschwandtner:

*"Problems are nothing but wake-up calls for **creativity**."*

Team Discussion

Are you still dealing with some of the same problems you dealt with last year? If so, what are they? And why haven't they been solved?

Does your team proactively or reactively solve problems? If your team is mostly reactive, how can you become more proactive?

What are your biggest decision-making challenges, and what can you do to overcome them as a team?

Challenges

Individual Challenge: What problems are you trying to prevent? What steps can you take to ensure you make the time to do it?

Team Challenge: Identify a problem that needs fixing and use the methodology to solve it. This does not have to be done in a single meeting!

Creativity and Ideation

A team must step away from the day-to-day and take a fresh approach to creating new products and services and providing solutions to existing processes.

Author's Thoughts

All good teams need to devise strategies to accomplish work. Given the complexities in the workplace, these strategies need to be creative and go beyond what we have typically done. Creativity involves using imagination and vision to come up with new ways of doing things or creating new products/services. Ideation is the generation of new thoughts or ideas that creativity puts into application. Both ideation and creativity require us to tap into a different part of the brain than we would usually use with problem solving. Most of us are stronger in problem solving because that is a major way in which we are taught to get work done. Problems arise, and we solve them. But we typically don't put as much time into figuring out new ways to approach these problems. When we are in a time crunch, we typically move quickly, and creativity requires a significant amount of time to think.

Creativity and Ideation

> **Creativity:** *Using imagination and vision to come up with new ways of doing things or creating new products/services.*

> **Ideation:** *The generation of new thoughts or ideas that creativity puts into application. Leads to the creation of something innovative.*

Why Are Creativity and Ideation So Important?

As with problem solving and decision making, we are talking about two separate but connected concepts. When combined, creativity and ideation support both innovation and problem solving. Ideas are the backbone of innovation. Without them, business cannot grow or be sustained.

Fostering a culture of creativity and ideation empowers teams to freely share ideas without fear of failure, iterate rapidly, improve idea output, and have a new perspective on familiar challenges. It creates a culture where going beyond the *"normal"* is the norm.

British economist John Maynard Keynes said, *"The difficulty lies not so much in developing new ideas as in escaping from old ones."* Which begs the question, can innovative thinking be learned? When we think of innovators, who do we think of? Maybe people like Steve Jobs, Jeff Bezos, Richard

Branson, and Pierre Omidyar. We don't typically think of the guy in the cubicle to the left of us. But what if we did? What if you had a culture where when someone asked you who the most innovative or creative person you could think of was, you immediately thought of John from the cubicle next to you?

The Ideation Challenge

One of the biggest misunderstandings about ideation is the thought that the more ideas we have, the more innovative we'll be. If you think about that for a moment, you'll probably come to the conclusion that this really isn't true. The whole purpose of ideation is to come up with not a bunch of random ideas, but that one big idea that has the potential to change things. Most organizations actually have a lot of ideas, but making even a single one successful is truly a challenge. So rather than just holding ideation sessions to generate a plethora of ideas, a more effective use of time would be to have a purpose and focus those sessions on not only capturing all currently existing ideas, but then also clarifying and then prioritizing them in a way that allows for the best use of resources.

I have found in my work with teams that the skills it takes to innovate can be learned. And since these skills can be learned, why aren't we doing more to foster their growth in ourselves, our teams, our departments, and our organizations?

Five Key Skills for Innovation

1) **Questioning** allows innovators to challenge the status quo and consider new possibilities.
2) **Observing** helps innovators detect small details—in the activities of customers, suppliers, and other companies—that suggest new ways of doing things.
3) **Networking** permits innovators to gain radically different perspectives from individuals with diverse backgrounds.
4) **Experimenting** prompts innovators to relentlessly try out new experiences, take things apart, and test new ideas.
5) **Associational thinking** is about drawing connections among questions, problems, or ideas from unrelated fields; it is triggered by questioning, observing, networking, and experimenting and is the catalyst for creative ideas.

At the end of this section, take some time to do the individual challenge and assess your innovation skills.

Creative Moments

When was the last time you had a lightbulb go off when you were thinking about a problem or trying to come up with an idea? When you do, in simple terms, your brain experiences a spike right before the answer comes to you, and there is a connection to other parts of the brain to finally put everything together in a new way.

So, how do we get to this aha moment? We have to be sure to ask the right questions, look for numerous potential explanations, and really look from multiple perspectives. We need to step back and see things from a different approach. This often requires being in a different location, participating in brainstorming sessions, working with new people, inviting in people with backgrounds diverse from yours, and imagining possibilities. It also means taking away your initial thoughts and first impressions. To do this, I often ask teams to provide a list of potential solutions or ideas. I then take this list away from them and say, "These are no longer options; now create a new list." They will often say that I am crippling them, but I am actually doing just the opposite: I am enabling them to go beyond the less creative place their brain first took them. They are then able to experience new ways to create value. Taking away your initial thoughts really makes you dig deep and find ways to challenge your brain to emerge with innovative concepts that you get when you really exhaust some mental energy. Others get their most unique thoughts when they are sitting in the car, taking a walk, viewing art, listening to music, and so on. So some ideas just come when the brain is not really even trying. I believe so much that the environment matters in the type of ideas you generate that in our spaces in Cleveland, Ohio, we have a "work" space that looks just a bit cooler than your typical office; the "fun," colorful, interactive aMAZEing Teams space; and a "relax" space that is a superinviting loft that looks like you are in the comfort of your living room. We have three separate environments created for our teams to have moments where ideas spark.

But let's go a step further. It takes more than just understanding what creative and innovative thinking is ... you need to do something with it and work to also develop it in others. So, I'll leave you with this question: *What will you do?*

Team Discussion

What was one creative idea or aha moment you had in the last twelve months? Describe the experience.

What are you doing to develop innovative skills in yourself and your team?

How can your team help to foster a creative and innovative culture at your organization?

Challenges

Individual Challenge: Rate yourself on these five key skills for innovation. Spend some time recognizing aspects of yourself that you need to intentionally develop/strengthen and identify ways you can do that.

Skills	Rating 1= Weakness; 5=Strength	Action to Develop Skills
Questioning	1 2 3 4 5	
Observing	1 2 3 4 5	
Networking	1 2 3 4 5	
Experimenting	1 2 3 4 5	
Associational Thinking	1 2 3 4 5	

Team Challenge: Set aside five minutes in your next team meeting time to work on developing your creativity. This could be a game, a problem to solve, and so on. Use your imagination!

Final Message to Organizations and Teams

Author's Final Thoughts

Increasing your effectiveness as a team member and/or leader through the seven attributes will require a significant amount of energy, time, and resources. Consider these three final thoughts as ways to sustain the momentum of your team's journey.

1. Intentionality leads to exponential changes.

> You must be deliberate by making improvement in these areas a priority, taking sufficient time to explore your current state, desired state, and how to best close any gaps with creative strategies. Creating designated time to work and plan is critical. If you do not *intentionally* set aside time alone and with your team, you will not see the kind of results you desire and the kind of results that are possible.

2. Consistency and commitment yield noticeable positive differences.

> Remember, team building is something that should be an ongoing focus, not just a once-a-year event. But before you embark on any improvement strategy, be sure to gain the commitment of your team. We have a saying that change imposed is change opposed. Be sure you give your team ownership by including them in the process, and then set aside consistent time together to focus on each attribute throughout the year.

3. You optimize what you measure.

> As you identify your priorities for improvement, be sure you have a way to measure how successful you've been. These measures can be objective, such as how many team meetings achieved the desired outcomes, or subjective, such as an anonymous survey that rates the level of trust your team members have for one another. However you do it, remember that our human nature leads us to work the way we are measured, so be sure you have

specific measures in place for your team to work toward. Finally, remember not to get caught up in metrics alone, but rather, put the focus on the intention behind them—to make your team as **cohesive**, **productive**, and **resilient** as it can be.

What will your team achieve?

Stick together to *produce results, recover from challenges, and eliminate complacency.*

Frequently Asked Questions

We hear from teams all across the country. Here are a few of the most common challenges we hear about and some insight into how to address them.

Question: I have a lot of turnover on my team. What can I do?

Answer: Turnover is a major challenge teams across the country are facing. In our work, we are seeing workers stay in their jobs just three to four years. This means they could have ten to fifteen jobs over the course of their working lives! So it is no wonder that teams are experiencing higher turnover rates than ever before. The first thing to do is to get to the root cause of the turnover. Is it simply because your team is made up of primarily entry-level employees who are not interested in staying with the company long-term, or is it something more? Look at exit interview data and ask current employees for insight. Maybe it is something that you can affect or control, and maybe it isn't. But you won't know what to focus on unless you first know the reason for the turnover.

In the meantime, here are a few suggestions to consider:

- Make your employees' experience as part of your team as meaningful as it can be. Go back to the section on appreciation and make sure you are showing your appreciation for your employees in a sincere and meaningful way.
- Be sure your team understands and is committed to your team and organizational goals.
- Look for opportunities to coach/mentor your team.
- Give them challenging work, but don't overload them. You don't want them to burn out, but you don't want them to feel like their skills are not being utilized either.
- Ensure you are empowering them to take ownership of their work.

Question: There is only one person on my team who is really causing the trouble. How should I handle it?

Answer: This is a tricky one. In most cases the manager should take the person aside and work with him or her to understand the root cause and correct the behavior. After all, it may be something he or she is not even aware of doing. Depending on the person's awareness of the behavior, then the correct course of action can be taken. If the person is unaware, the first step is working on alerting him or her to the behavior and the impact it is having on the team and then work out strategies to manage it. If the person is aware and just doesn't care, understanding the root cause of the behavior is key, and then focus on regulating it. After all, sometimes people go through difficult periods at work and in their personal lives that may be affecting their behavior. These things must be taken into consideration when working to change the behavior. Work with the individual to set goals for improving or eliminating the behavior. Once he or she is aware of what needs to change, you need to follow whatever standard protocols your organization has set forth. This could include verbal warnings, write-ups, suspensions, and so on. Whatever behavioral goals you agree upon, make sure to include them in employee performance evaluations if possible.

Question: How do I get my team back on track after a major setback?

Answer: Unfortunately, setbacks are a natural part of business, and *all* teams have them. Don't feel you've failed because of these setbacks. The first thing you need to do is openly and honestly acknowledge and discuss the setback with your team. This goes back to trust. You won't be doing your team any favors by pretending or sugar-coating. If they find out (and they will!) that you've been less than honest with them, you will lose their respect and ultimately their trust. It is also important not to place the blame on any one person. You are a team, and no one should be singled out to take the blame for something going wrong. If the breakdown did indeed happen because of the actions of a single person, you should address it with the individual one-on-one, not in a team setting. Once you have acknowledged the setback, you must work together to find out why it occurred and what the impact was. Then go through the problem-solving steps to come up with a solution and put together a detailed plan to repair any damage and overcome the obstacle or setback in your way. Be sure to take time to discuss what you learned and what will you do to prevent this type of setback from happening in the future. By facing setbacks head-on and working together as a team to resolve and learn from them, your team is practicing resilience and will become stronger as a result of it.

Question: I have a new team and don't think we are off to a great start. What can I do?

Answer: Henry Ford said it best: "Coming together is a beginning; keeping together is progress; working together is success." Building a new team is never easy. Different personalities, backgrounds, and skills are all factors that play into how well a team gels together. As a leader, the first thing you need to do is ensure that you have the right people. Assess your goals and then make sure you have the personalities and skills you need to be successful. Then get to know at a deeper level who is on your team. That means taking the time to get to know everyone. Remember the platinum rule of appreciation? This is the perfect time to ensure you create a culture of appreciation right from the start. Team members will be trying to figure out norms and each other, so be sure to set your expectations up front. Be clear about any standard processes and preferences you have. Model the behavior you wish to see in your team and be consistent. Remember, you are trying to establish credibility and trust early on. Finally, it is never too early to begin to integrate consistent and focused time for team-building activities. Be sure to close the communication loop by asking your team for feedback and suggestions; this not only gives you insight in how/what to improve, but gives them ownership into the success of the team.

About Improve Consulting and Training Group

Improve Consulting and Training Group, LLC, is a personal and professional development consulting firm with extensive experience in leadership development and continuous improvement. We are based in Cleveland, Ohio, but provide services globally.

Tagline

Empowering you to exceed your potential.

Vision

To "improve" the workplace through education, strategy, and team engagement.

Mission

To provide high-quality, customized personal and professional development services.

Service Commitment

We make processes more efficient and the people and teams who work on them more effective.

Improve Consulting and Training Group offers many services to increase the effectiveness and productivity of your team in a fun and engaging way. Improve provides training, team building, coaching, and consulting services.

Our team of professionals can also come to your location to deliver competent strategies and proven solutions to overcome many of the problems that your organization may face.

Our company is eager to share our culture-changing methods with you and partner to help you exceed your potential.

To further support our clients, Improve also provides versatile meeting and office spaces for teams and training, team assessments, group and meeting facilitation, a loft space for private team lunches catered by a local chef, and administrative services during your visit—or invite us to bring our skills and services on the road and visit you!

Since 2006, the firm has been providing services to clients in the following key areas:

- Hands-on Workshops and Seminars
- Meeting Facilitation
- Train-the-Trainer Workshops for Facilitators
- Curriculum Design and Development
- Process Improvement Training and Consulting
- Individual and Group Coaching/Development
- Program Assessments and Evaluations
- Simulations and Team Building
- Strategic and Operational Planning
- Succession Planning/Executive Development
- Facility Usage for Team Retreats
- Young Professionals Development
- Keynote and Guest Speaking

We have added value to hundreds of individual leaders and teams and would certainly like to see how we can add value to yours.

About the Book

aMAZEing Organizational Teams is a guide for improving group workplace dynamics. It is based on the aMAZEing Team Building Experience located in Cleveland, Ohio, where teams navigate through a maze of highly interactive indoor mental challenges based on seven attributes of healthy, productive teams. This body of work brings those experiences to the reader to help individuals and teams in any organization successfully navigate the complexities that increase productivity, cohesion, and resilience, leading to more effective engagement. This book serves as a team action planning workbook and discussion, walking the reader through these seven critical attributes. Teams are given guidance on how to (1) build and/or increase trust, (2) foster an environment of appreciation, (3) manage meetings to productive outcomes, (4) deliver robust solutions through improved problem-solving and decision-making techniques, (5) master the elements required for improved communication, (6) manage healthy behavioral interactions, (7) all while continuously generating new ideas and thinking creatively about ways to improve process and products.

Edwards Brothers Malloy
Thorofare, NJ USA
June 17, 2016